SHAW

ORLANDA SHAW
SHAW

FROM BUMS TO BENTLEYS

S h a w Entertainment, LLC
250 Palm Coast Parkway, NE
STE 157
Palm Coast, Florida 32137

Shawentertainmentllc157@gmail.com

Charleston, SC
www.PalmettoPublishing.com

SHAW

Copyright © 2023 by Orlanda Shaw

All rights reserved.

No portion of this book may be reproduced, stored in a retrieval system, or transmitted in any form by any means—electronic, mechanical, photocopy, recording, or other—except for brief quotations in printed reviews, without prior permission of the author.

First Edition

Hardcover ISBN: 979-8-8229-1575-6
Paperback ISBN: 979-8-8229-1576-3
eBook ISBN: 979-8-8229-1577-0

ABOUT THE AUTHOR

My name is *Orlanda Shaw*, born May 15, 1975, at *Detroit Receiving* into a world that gave 2-shits about my ass! If I had any spiritual control over my birth, I would have dived headfirst back into the womb like a time-capsule and got the fuck on! I was destined for disaster the day I learned the meaning of it. You see, as a child you really don't know that love is coming from those who are supposed to embrace and teach you the true meaning of it. It's all mentally connected and you catch on pretty fast to the difference between love and hate.

Without going into too much of my dialogue, I just want to give you a heads up that this journey I'm about to take you on is not apples and pears... you know... something sweet... tasteful. My life was bitter... broken, filled with hate at a tender age. I'm honestly lucky, through all the turn of events I'm here to tell my story. I guess that was the plan all the time. Like Jesus, I was a sacrifice. Though there is no real comparison to the Godly greatness of the man to what I went through. I have accepted the fact that I had to go through it, so that I could stand here today to tell my story with the hopes that it encourages and help those who may have been through, going through, or didn't make it through all the trauma I had at the hands of the one person who I never saw the evilness that dwelled behind closed doors.

Now, here I am, blessed to see the age of 48. I am grateful to have reached greatness for the most part. So, I invite you to ride shot gun through my life's journey. I can't promise many of you can stomach some of the content with the fact that this shit is far from fiction…it's my reality. But what I pray it does is attach healing to your lives whether you're the victim or the volunteer. This is, and will always be, one of the hardest projects I've ever done in my life, confronting evil face-to-face….

You know I have always wondered where my mom came up with the name *Orlanda*. It wasn't like we were the kind of family that took trips to *Disney World*, that happen to be in Orlando Florida. But I assure you, that wasn't the kind of life me and my siblings were born into. We came out the womb fending for ourselves. Abuse? I don't know if that word can fit the profile of what me and my siblings endured. No silver spoon here, baby. We pretty much raised ourselves after losing our only opportunity as kids to have what many around us called family. So, I don't have a fairytale story to tell you as I introduce you to the chapters of my fucked-up life. I just know that everything I experienced from the day I was born was a test of my sanity. So, inviting you into my personal space right now is not something I do in my day-to-day life. In other words, this here is a given. Though I was born and raised in Detroit, the streets I grew up in treated me fucked up. So, as I spin the wheel on who would have been the next mufucka in line to take advantage of me, I had to learn the hard way what my mission was in life and what I went through was destined for. It was being blessed with the power to heal, help give hope and peace to others. How? By telling my truth with the hopes that it may bring harmony, strength, and the courage one would need to share their story. This is one of the many steps for healing to begin. My story is to take the focus off me while sharing the strength I have that got me through it with you. Forgiving yourself first is the ONLY WAY to forgive those who know not what they do… And that's FACTS.

As the Author of how my journey took me from a bum to a Bentley, it doesn't change the fact that I'm a Shaw… No matter what clothes you rock or what car you drive… Never forget where you came from and I promise you, you will never forget that what you went through can be the roadmap to save others.

Enjoy this read…

DEDICATIONS

To my wonderful son, Eshante' Shaw.
I hope this book inspires you to achieve your dreams.
To Cedric Dorcas, my rock and greatest supporter.
You keep me reaching for the stars.
Thank you for believing in my dreams and helping me to achieve them.

LEFT TOP: My Sister Marlena Shaw & Me: Orlanda Shaw
RIGHT TOP: Mom Geraldine Shaw & My Brother James Shaw III

IN MEMORY OF

My Mother, Geraldine Shaw, My Father, James Shaw Jr, My Sister, Marlena Shaw and Younger Brother, James Shaw III. May my loved ones Rest In Peace, for you will always be a part of my soul. Though I feel you are here in spirit, you are truly missed and never forgotten. I know you all are smiling down from heaven, watching over me and protecting me.

This is for you!

TABLE OF CONTENTS

About the Author · v
Dedications · ix
In Memory Of · ix
Fucked Before 4 · xv

1 "Hostile" · 1
2 Why Us? · 6
3 Why Me? · 11
4 Thrift Store R-Kelly · · · · · · · · · · · · · · · · · · 14
5 A Reality Check Moment · · · · · · · · · · · · · · 16
6 Tell Me Anything · 18
7 Cooking & Clean-Ting · · · · · · · · · · · · · · · · 20
8 I'm Look'n At The Front Door · · · · · · · · · · 26
9 On Like Donkey Kong · · · · · · · · · · · · · · · · 29
10 "Living In Fear" · 33
11 The Ugly Duckling · · · · · · · · · · · · · · · · · · · 36
12 "NO NEW FRIENDS" "PUSHED TO A POINT OF
   NO RETURN" · 39
13 "Victims Of The System" · · · · · · · · · · · · · · 46

14	"Love Don't Pay The Bills"	51
15	"Make That Money…Don't Let The Money Make U…"	54
16	"I Ain't No Killa, But Don't Push Me"	59
17	Don't Test My Gangsta	63
18	"Poppa Was A Playa"	67
19	"Flesh of my Flesh, Bone of my Bone"	71
20	"Ghetto Love Story"	75
21	"I Had A Dream"	78

FUCKED BEFORE 4

Right now, I'm struggling with which turn of events of my life was the most fucked up growing up. Without disclosing my storyline of which one of me and my siblings got fucked over the worst emotionally, sexually, and physically, well shit…I can't honestly say which of the three was the most traumatic. But, one thing fasho, two things for certain, it was at the hands of the same muthafuckas that vowed to take care of us.

The first phase of my life was far from a box of chocolates. I would say it was more like a garbage can filled with maggots! *Picture that*! Kicked down a flight of stairs without touching one before hitting the bottom, to being locked in a basement for days at a time on some dumb-ass-looking-for-socks mission! Stay woke because a bitch is just getting started!

Being molested by my Auntie's "Love Child" every time she would exit the home, leaving me and my siblings behind to fend for ourselves. Now that I think back on that shit, I don't know what could have been going through that niggas mind to have any kind of desire to fuck with a child barely old enough to spell her own name. Tossed into foster care … a ward of the State, a muhfucka could've turned the wheel on our ass at any given time and had us in a whole trafficking ring! *Three kids… equals three checks…* That bitch wasn't turning no wheel, she flip'n coins! She had the three of us in a choke hold and every day I spent in that home, locked up in our bedroom, I couldn't fuckn' breathe. I came to realize at an early age that death been after me since I was born.

Every time I thought I had dodged it, that same evil spirit somehow found its way to snatch the closest person next to me. I had so many questions to ask God. I cried many nights, wondering if I was ever heard. How can someone so young, so innocent, fall so hard when they could barely stand on their own two feet long enough to walk against the wind? I was forced into adulthood. What the fuck was being a kid even like? Barbie dolls, Sesame Street, ABC's and 123's were nonexistent for me. The game of Monopoly was monopolized. I went from Park Place to Boardwalk and bitch you better have my rent.

I bypassed bullshit to bricks, once I learned that I held the key to my reality the whole time. I was forced to push that pain aside and slap a band-aide over my wounds. I had to get it how I lived, then go back and holler at those who tried to push my face in the sand. Though this game of chess had a different set of rules, I'm the Queen-B bitch. One of the most powerful pieces that move accordingly. Checkmate Bitch! This is how it's played… If I fuck with you, I FUCKS *with* you. There is no in between.

The picture that was once splattered on my wall, is now worth more than one of Picasso's best creations. Priceless. No more pro-wings and Payless sandals hanging off the back of my heels. I'm coming with Red Bottom Louboutin prints in muthafuckas backs. Though I was once lost, now found, I support the struggle and pity of stupidity. Surviving this game of my life in the streets of Detroit was real. *I'm a Shaw!* That's worth more than the diamond on my finger and the *Cuban Links* around my neck. I see the fake before its wrapped in plastic, the wolves approaching in sheep's clothing, that's a given.

From a *Bum to a Bentley*, how about I got two of them! I worked hard as fuck to earn and own everything I have. So, walk with me through each turn of events in my life, every page that's flipped and every chapter that's read. It will leave an unforgettable piece of me behind. If you're reading this book, I assure you, you're one of the lucky ones. This here is an unforgettable truth, that is so real, it raises the question of fiction, yet it tastes like reality. So, as I continue to tickle your palette, allow me to introduce myself.… *Orlanda Shaw*, A Rebel with a never-ending story.

1
"HOSTILE"

When I say I was in one of those deep fucking sleeps this particular time *Evillene* (A nickname I gave my "Aunt Karen" from the black version movie *The Wiz*) was on some menopause shit. Old ass, always trying to find a reason to fuck me and my siblings up over the dumbest shit. I swear on everything we regretted the day we knocked on her door. She found out we were up for grabs after my mom lost her parental rights. Cha-Ching! Dollar signs was all she saw. She didn't want us for the greater good or to do the right thing by us. We were cash cows... dass it.

"BITCH! GET YO' PISSY ASS UP OFF MY MUTHAFUCKING MATTRESS!"

She hoovered over me as I struggled to open my eyes trying to wake the fuck up! I came too quick feeling myself drenched in my own piss as it streamed up my back like an upside-down waterfall leaving me cold and uncomfortable. That wasn't what bounced me back into my fucked-up reality though. It was what I was soon to endure at the hands of someone so treacherous… so evil that had me shook.

"I'm sorry Aunnn…" I tried to force the words of an apology out before she pushed me face first into my mattress full of piss followed up by beating my ass. As if me having to taste the putrid sensation of my own urine choking me like a room filled with soot from a burning fire. The fact that I was punished so severely for something out of my control, I knew right at that very moment what me and my siblings was up against for the duration of the time we were forced to spend under her roof.

If I wasn't her punching bag for the day, my baby brother would take my place. I hated her with a deadly passion. My fantasies of how I could kill her and get away with it was as vivid as a court case TV Series. I could see it unfold right before my eyes. As a matter of fact, I still have those same desires to ice the bitch every time I see her in my adult-life once I finally got on. But, let me stop thinking ahead. Though I was a kid trying to figure shit out, my sister Marlena, which happened to be the second oldest, caught hell there also. The devil stayed busy. I could never understand what we did so wrong to be treated so cruel. It was like we were paying for our parent's sins. We were fucking kids without parents. Passed off to family members that should have been the next best thing.

But I guess that wasn't in "God's plan", which is probably one of the reasons why I'm not as religious as I should be. I grew tired of asking that man floating in the sky to rescue me and my siblings. As I sat my ass there waiting to be heard, the beatings kept coming. I stopped praying and started paying for every mood swing or menstruation Aunt Karen was on at the time. In other words, I gave up and just endured the shit. I started utilizing the skill of imagining that one day I would be saved from the wrath of this woman and her son (which is a whole *nothah'* nightmare that turned into a dream). *Imagine that.*

Now, I wasn't the only one who had to deal with this bitch on a daily basis. My sister, Marlena, had to dodge bullets, too! None of us was able to help one another; our feet were shackled. I learned quick she couldn't do shit to help me or Lil Ron Jr which was my baby brother under me. Now, don't ask me where my oldest brother was while all of this was going on. He was the only slave that didn't get caught by Massah (Auntie Karen). Kunta Kinte escaped while our ass got, got. He was in the streets doing his thang, falling through to see us whenever the moon was pink, but fuck it… I'm not gon' trip on that shit right now. But I am a realist, and this here is real shit. We saw him when we saw him which wasn't as often. Street niggas don't pay random house visits; they're married to the streets to like a jealous bitch that can't breathe without riding her nigga's dick 23 out of 24 hours a day.

My brother Desmond, aka Dezi, was obligated to the game like some Bloods and Crips shit. We weren't priority in his life during that time and for that reason alone I would always fight against having to remember that one seat at the dinner table not taken to be able to block food that was constantly thrown in our face… (a metaphor). But that's what it felt like whenever I looked for protection…he just wasn't there.

Now, I'm not saying this to say he didn't love us. In his eyes he was comfortable that we were with family and had a roof over our heads. So rare visits weren't missed. So, to not hate him for not being there I forced myself to protect his reason for not being there… I guess.

Anyhow, we just never knew what box that bitch was gone jump out of. We just had to stay alert and take cover whenever the volcano erupted. As much as we tried to adapt to the mood swings and the ass whooping and the wild goose chases. As a kid, for me… I just had to stay in character for the most part. I could wear a smile while crying inside. Shit after so long, became normal. I was on punishment so much that it became a normal routine, writing bullshit 3,000 times or being locked in a basement to look for socks that didn't exist became a walk in the park.

What the bitch didn't know was I was working on an exit plan that started right after Marlena ran away! I knew once she was gone shit was going to get even worst for a bitch. There we were, just me and my baby brother James left there to fend for ourselves… The shit was a losing battle that had no wins. In other words, we were fucked… royally.

2
WHY US?

Have you ever been in a situation where you found yourself hopeless and afraid? I'm talking about where you couldn't do shit to save or help the one you loved? Well, I have. This day was like a movie scene out of one of the Freddy Krueger's film series, *Nightmare On Elm Street*... To have to watch this *Lady From Hell* (Auntie Karen) chase my baby brother under the bed with a broomstick and commence to jabbing his small petite frame with the broom's wooden end of the handle in order to get him to come from under the bed! What the bitch didn't realize, being that she was on 10 like a drug addict whose system was on fire, I had to ask myself... *"Was she trying to kill him?"* At least that's what his cries of pain sounded like to me!

It was hurtful to be forced to sit in a corner as I watched her repeatedly jabbing him. I was shaking and crying under my breath to avoid her from turning the broom stick on me! Those excruciating sounds of him crying out in pain, I can still hear to this very day. I just sat there, *just fucking helpless*. All due to sneaking out the house to go to a store to get something to eat, from starving, from hunger pains. That didn't move her spirit to be sympathetic towards the situation at all. After she wore herself out poking him with the broom, she forced him to stay underneath the bed the remainder of the day and throughout the night.

I guess I couldn't reason with the situation back then; her rules were fucking ridiculous! Hell, in her home we got smacked around or put on punishment if we ate a sandwich a certain way! It was on the hot summer days when all the kids were playing outside. Now ask me where was me and my brother? Eventually she ended up calling the social worker over our case and had him removed from her home.

Try being on punishment three months out of a summer forced to stare out the window watching normal kids in normal family situations exist in their constructed elements. While we sat in a tight ass room, we both shared three to three-and-a-half summer months out of the year on punishment! Reliving this shit makes me want to go beat her ass, I swear on everything though I'm grown and gone from that dungeon.

I felt like I spent most of my life locked up in a women's state prison where I heard horror stories of where women being locked in these tight ass cells with their bunkies and no toilet. They had asked these stick-stuck-up-in-their-ass guards where some of them were the same age as them, if not younger, to use the bathroom. My aunt created the rule to let you hold your piss and shit between your ass cheeks for hours on some ego-stroking shit till you damn near had to let loose in your wastebasket! Of course, that would have led to another ass whooping. And let me NOT forget having to write three and four-line sentences, three and four thousand times. *Can you imagine how long it takes to write a three-to-four-line sentence 4,000 times?* Hell, I was around 10/11 years old and lil' man was pushing up on six or seven as far as I can remember at the time. Though we were both fuck'n clueless. There was food in the house, but the bitch kept the shit locked up.

For one thing I must give *Evilene* her props when it came to the kitchen tho', she was a helluva cook and she took time to teach me when she wasn't on one of her bi-polar breakdowns. So, there was some good in her that minimized the bad, which was the only thing about living under her roof that had some essence to it. I feel like my brother was just scared to come out the room this specific day. I can't call it; it could have been the sun shining and he wanted to enjoy it, being that we were unfortunately always locked in darkness. So he snuck his ass out the window which was on the side of the house and he ended up having to walk through the alley and later regretted it. I wasn't aware at the time that my Uncle Reggie saw my brother sneak out, both my aunt and uncle walked in together and all hell broke loose on baby bro ass.

So, this shit became real at an early age. I could vividly remember spending whole summers locked in that damn room. So, to find the first opportunity when you thought no one was paying attention to sneak out the window to get just a taste of freedom was a given! I get it, I blame that snitch-ass uncle trying to get some brownie points for getting him fucked up! And you know what, **RIP Uncle**, but I never looked at him the same that day my brother found himself at the wrath of my aunt for just a few minutes of sunshine and some candy.

Just going back down memory lane on this specific incident, which we shared many. I could honestly hear the stabbing noises puncturing his rib cage, stomach…omg, to have to revisit this is bringing me to tears! Not just because of what she did… but the fact that her reasoning was unreasonable. This was years later, which we will revisit that as my story develops.

One thing was for sure was how bitter-sweet it was when the state snatched him up out of there. Though I didn't like seeing none of my siblings leave me behind, I don't know what was worse… them getting beat while being helpless where I couldn't do anything to save them from the abuse, or me being left behind. One thing I was forced to accept at that point was like *Pac* spit in his lyrics… *"It was me against the world"* … Flat the fuck out.

In other words, there was no need to indulge into her evil acts at this point. I've expressed enough to make me sick to my stomach. So, moving on, is what we gone do right nah…

I had an exit plan which was getting the fuck on when a bitch least expected it. I knew I couldn't just walk out her front door while she's having her morning coffee on the living room couch. I just had to stay one step ahead of that shit. A bitch had to have somewhere to go. With my brother doing him and my dad was God-knows-where, I had limited resources. So, in other words, I had to catch those hands until shit got smoother.

3
WHY ME?

While some kids lived normal lives where they could utilize diaries, get counseling or outsource other physiological tools overseen by therapist to escape from the madness that exist in their lives, I had constant reminders of how ugly my life was at such a young age. One day in particular was the day my auntie son, that we called O, decided he wanted to fuck with a minor. Yeah, the nightmare got worse. And guess who the minor was…. A nine-year-old-still-in-her-most-precious-innocent-phase-in-her-life; me. The way he would slide into my space when my auntie would leave the house was treacherous! I mean, what could I do?

My aunt had a short fuse when it came to me; it didn't fucking matter. I was stuck in this world where candy and bubblegum were more like acid and fentanyl. I was bound to overdose on fucking life and everything it was made of. It wasn't like having a normal life where people who cared read you bedtime stories and took you on camping trips, or hell, THE FUCKING PARK! I missed out on the swing-sets and the Belle Isle Giant Slide. If we didn't build our own play yard experience, we settled for a fantasy. The reality of my situation right then was my innocence being snatched right from up under me like a filthy rug I was forced to lay on and get trampled over.

I felt violated. I had to lay there while this man, not a boy, not a kid playing house while our parents were upstairs playing cards and listening to Teena Marie. This was a scene in the movie where you could hear his belt buckle hit the headboard while he climbs up on top of me and take care of his *"bitness..."*, in my Celie voice from the scene in the movie *The Color Purple*. That was some dark ass shit going on in that movie. To think being violated back in those days where grown ass musty fucking men slept and enslaved young black girls was legal?

Not to mention they was like a product on the stock market that was sold to them to do what they wanted when they wanted; sick! That's how I felt at first… nauseous. Every time this dude climbed on top of me or slung me around like his sexual princess in filthy ballerina shoes, fucked with me…*at first*. Some things that are out of your control and you find yourself giving into the control. It's a weird kind of attraction.

I mean, being that my aunt was addicted to Bingo nights and a few drinks enough to get a buzz, that surprisingly wasn't what brought on ass whoopings. That was one thing about that bitch, she wanted to be sober and fully aware when it came to beating our asses. It was like a workout; something she enjoyed. What other reason did she have? It wasn't like we were bad, spoiled rotten kids! I can't recall ever giving her a solid reason for punishing and beating us the way she did without pause or reason.

I hardly ever made her that fucking angry to pick up a broom stick, an extension cord or whatever she could get her hands on! *Mid-Evil* or something even more sinister… *Eveline*… was the adopted name I came up with after watching that treacherous scene in the black version of the movie *"The Wiz"*.

Now, there I was left there in her home to fend for myself without my siblings who would sometimes shield the abuse not to protect me, but it had its way in subliminally placing me in the back of the line of fire. This was my way, in my mind, of avoiding getting burnt. Being the only one left there to wake up into a nightmare or a dream was the scary part. But it was the reality I was forced into.

So, this was where I learned the true meaning of *"If you can't beat them join 'em…"* Now you tell me how fucked my life really was, when instead of becoming the victim, I found myself becoming a volunteer.

4
THRIFT STORE R-KELLY

You know, I knew I couldn't hide from a fucked-up day living here with *Evilene* and *Chester-The-Child-Molester*, so I had to go into survival mode by faking it till making it. In other words, on those days when my aunt would switch characters in my make-believe imaginary mind from *Evilene* to *Auntie-Em* (which the good witch bad witch was rare). Hell, her ass was hardly ever soft as cotton, but those moments when she was, I would really try to connect with that side of her. I think that's when I started analyzing and studying muhfuckas. It was a well-needed skill that I learned early on which saved me from a lot of potentially deadly situations in my life.

Now don't get me wrong, I wasn't that damn good. But, for the most part those antennas went up when necessary, in some close encounter situations. So, for that reason alone, enduring the shit I went through living under her roof had it's good, bad, and ugly moments. But those were called tools. Tools that I could carry around in the back of my mind and pull them out like a red beam attached to my hip and lock in on my target.

I wasn't a killer, nor did I pursue muhfuckas for the better good on every occasion when accessible. I just learned how to protect myself and those who I cared about by living dangerously and going through some shit so that I could never get sideswiped when my blinders are on. Like my aunt's son, O…I'll use him as an example.

When you're a child being taken advantage of like I was sexually, at a young age we as young girls growing into women often become curious and weirdly aroused. That was me. I started finding myself liking his touch, his smell his tongue gracing my private parts after a while. It was a feeling that I didn't even know my body withheld. I just knew that day he brought something out of my *va-jay-jay* came unexpectedly and I liked it.

I started to like it so much that I craved for him in a way that I knew was wrong. But I was bored, needed the attention and something to fucking do to take my mind off the fact that I was stuck. I had to accept my fate even though eventually like breaking out of prison, I would find a way out. But in the meantime, … I was going to ride this wave in this sea of sharks. I was already drowning, so fuck it!

5
A REALITY CHECK MOMENT

Clearly this is not a fairytale fucking story. I did end up saying something to Evilene about her *Thrift-Store R. Kelly* son who was careful enough to slide his limp ass dick in my asshole to cover his tracks in case she came up with a reason to take me to a doctor for a checkup. I'll never forget that day. How foolish was I to think I would get some sympathy after revealing that shit. No wonder I waited so long. She had this blank stare at first. I couldn't really read it 'till she yelled out to him, forcing him to come into the room where I sat across from her. I don't know what the fuck I was thinking to blow up his spot. Especially with the fact that I was starting to enjoy it!

I don't know whether I was feeling some type of way after seeing him fucking with other chicks or just wanting to end it by watching her fuck him up! Hell, I don't know…maybe I just needed the attention taken off of me long e'nuff to ride under the radar to make moves that would get me the fuck up out of there! None of that shit worked in my favor. She asked him did he do it and he gave her this blank stare with no response and walked the fuck off. No bottle thrown upside his head… No swift kick in his ass and not even a few harsh words like "You dirty muthafucka… how could you!" She just looks away in awe. It was emotionless.

There was sure favoritism and this weird fear of protection that gave me the fucking creeps. That's when I knew it wasn't going to end well for me or my siblings if we hadn't got the fuck on. But until courage meets fire, I had to sit on death row and wait out those long harsh and abusive years until whatever plan God had for me and my siblings was revealed. Damn, ya'll… I really didn't know if faith could protect me too much longer.

6
TELL ME ANYTHING

So, dig this. There was no angel with wings that would fly down and shield us from the ugly ducklings in our lives. Me and my siblings didn't have the kind of parents that asked us how our day was at school or snuck into our room as a *Tooth Fairy*, placing money under our pillow every time we lost a tooth.

Let me not forget during Christmas time when the malls were filled with joy, and you get to sit on *Santa's* lap where you get that once a year moment to tell him everything you want under your tree. Well, dude was in for a rude awakening. This was not a kodak moment for him. I wasn't the average kid that you can smile in my face, and I would roll out the red carpet for you. It's levels to that shit. I was sure after me there will be no other.

First off, I was a smart ass that didn't smile as much. So, after all the *"What do you want for Christmas Little Angel"* questions, he could have missed me with that shit! I was ready already a little irritated to have to stand in that line with all of them damn whining ass Caucasian and Chaldean kids. Not to mention it was so loud that his half-death-ass forced me to have to keep repeating myself. So, when I slid in this last comment, *"Look, dude don't play with me..."* and gave him this serious ass look, he smirked forcing his crooked beard to shift even more, waiting on me to return a smile as I sat on his lap with my arms folded mean-mug'n him. I should have known I was being hood-winked then, but I didn't want to chance him not getting my list together. He gave me a blank stare like...*"this bitch is serious..."*

I wasn't for the games. You tell me something, you better live up to it. Your word is everything and though some may get a pass every now and then, I don't forget that you tripped up. *"What comes out your mouth... you can't reach out and grab it back."* – Denzel Washington in the movie *Training Day* quoted....

One thing I learned as a kid was that we believe most of the things that we are told, especially coming from loved ones; *unless we're shown different.* Even then we can be fooled.

Overall, this myth became blatantly clear. Life is not like a box of chocolates for minorities; it's more like a box of charcoal, that once it's lit, you can easily get burned. Facts....

7
COOKING & CLEAN-TING

"*It's like a jungle sometimes* it makes me wonder wow I keep from going under…" As the bumping bass and lyrics from one of *Grand Master Flash & The Furious Five* song roared through the neighborhood, them lyrics was sketched into my soul; it was so real. It was like it was meant for me to hear that day.

There I was sitting by the window catching a warm breeze from the warm summer air blowing in. Of course, I was on punishment, which was so often that I started making make-believe that I was this girl locked in prison for a murder she did not commit. I was used to role-playing just to move time fast. That shit never worked tho'. It was like watching the clock tick slow. It was some days when I just didn't want to wake up into this jungle I pictured as a prison cell. There was no genuine love in this bitch. It was all skeptical.

I literally felt like I had nothing to wake up to, other than misery that loved my fucking company. But I can admit whenever my aunt would warm up to me wanting to be bothered by having me in her personal space, I shared the pleasure in enjoying cooking with her whenever she felt this desire to switch her heart from cold to warm. It wasn't like I had better things to do with my time being that I was on twenty-three-hour lock down. She would yell out, "GUARD! OPEN CELL 9!" LOL! Though this is just me living in my head, that's what it felt like for us. Prison. The crazy part was I didn't even have to know what prison felt like to describe what it seemed like.

Nevertheless, every now and then she would invite me into her personal space. I ate shit like that up! It's like any kind of attention I got while living with Evilene was as good as it gets. So, I embraced the cooking lessons on some grown women shit.

We made *collard greens with smoked turkey, yams, mac-n-cheese, leg-of-Lamb, cabbage, green beans, Mexican cornbread, Chitterlings...* And what was so fucking crazy was the fact that by us being on punishment for long periods at a time, I wasn't able to keep up with holidays like Easter, Halloween... Thanksgiving. The *ONLY* reason why Christmas was so vivid was because me and my younger brother grew some balls and was anxious and excited to see what was wrapped up in the gifts she had placed under the tree for us this one particular Christmas.

You probably know where I'm going with this story but anyways, the ringleader (myself) decided to try and peel open a few of our gifts just to take a peek, thinking I was that damn slick enough to not get caught. I mean, in my mind I felt I could cover our tracks by putting everything back where she had it. Hell, and after I had set everything back up the way it was it seemed good to me. I thought it was one of my best works honestly. That's why the saying "You don't get paid to think" …well, that saying was worded correctly. It was like she set traps for us, and my ass fell for the shit damn near every time. That's bitch missed her calling. She should have been a private investigator or some shit. It wasn't more than a second before that bitch beamed in on those gifts under the tree and noticed they'd been *messed wit*… (In my *Mista* voice from the movie *The Color Purple*…)

I don't really have to go into too much detail on what kind of ass whooping we endured that day. Just know it was just as brutal as all the others. And to top it off… She returned every last gift to the store just to extend the pain of punishment inflicted on us that night. That bitch was a she-Devil. I don't know what she endured growing up. I can only imagine how horrible my mom and her sibling's life could have been without having very little knowledge to back it up.

Enough reliving another fucked up chapter of living with Evilene and let me get back to some of the good that I walked away from after leaving that hellhole.

I was sharing what I experienced in the kitchen with the knock-off *Betty Crocker* back then. So hopefully it's understood as I move on to why I can't just walk away and not finish this thought of my one-on-one time with my aunt in the kitchen and why it has relevance. What I've uncovered with this experience was I found myself trying to swim to the top of this ocean like a bad nightmare where you're trying to run from a villain, and you find yourself slow motioning back into the same spot.

So, to assure you, I'm not exaggerating, after investing mentally in what I shared in these chapters hoping to release, move-on and heal from the nightmares of living under her roof, I found myself not having much good to say. But I had to be honest though; it was hard to share the lesson by the many turns of events that happened that I drowned it out. I ain't gon' lie, I could count on one or two fingers of the good nurturing moments I took with me once I got the fuck on. It wasn't a learning experience in life that many have missed out on growing up with having some knowledge on how to cook. That was one of the learning tools I could honestly say she shared with me that I was grateful for upon my exit.

It pains me to have something good to say being that our relationship till this very day haven't healed from our past. But I realize life is about forgiving, moving on… and taking the good with the bad and using it to make the right adjustments when necessary. I'm not going to hate on the plate. She can cook her ass off and I found this time with her to be somewhat peaceful for me. Though I had absolutely no desire to get off into the who cleaning *Shit-Lings* (Chitterlings) disgusting, this was a Southern-African American Entre that some black folks seemed to enjoy on the holidays. Cleaning them stinking mufuckas was a whole different animal. I wanted to bypass that to the desserts. The way she made her own breading for her Peach Cobbler was amazing to watch. It was all in the wrist and the rolling of the dough and butter. She was that bitch when it came to the flick of the wrist.

I had to admit, I really had this different level of respect with her that for once didn't have a dose of fear of being beaten. It was one of those moments I wish I shared with my mom. I missed her though this part of me that was drowning in resentment and disappointment for putting me and my siblings in harm's-way had its way of clouding my judgment. There was this hate that not only reflected personal hate, but the feeling of not being in our lives by choosing drugs and the street corners over us forced me to forget her instead of forgiving her; for she knew not what she'd done. I know this sounds Biblical, but sometimes to gain understanding of why my life was so fucked up I had to make shit make sense to move forward.

Anyhow, cooking with Evilene was a calm storm that never erupted in violence and abuse. I could honestly say that the kitchen may have been the safest place for us. Well, not as safe but I'll tap into that later.

Back to the kitchen... I would sometimes capture her crack what appeared to be a smile that had me letting my guard down just a little. The structure of her face never gave-way for a smile that I could remember, so it was hard to determine at that time what showing her teeth was for. Hell, I thought maybe she was looking for a toothpick or some shit when I noticed. But I was wrong after a minute of what happened shortly after.

I was the one that had a hard time letting my guard down. Mainly because I knew how fast that script would flip and I would be back in *Cell Block Hate* (my room with the small window to nowhere) ... I would have done damn near anything to stay out of there after being on punishment all those months! So, when she called out to the guard to unlock my cell to release the prisoner from the twenty-three-hour lock down for some recreational time, I was all fucking in.

8
I'M LOOK'N AT THE FRONT DOOR

Decisions...decisions...decisions...hummmm...
I'm shaking like a heroin addict right now. Though carelessly I use this term to express the emotions I was feeling right then as I had a clean break to the front door to escape this horror story of my life once and for all. I was scared az' fuck to make that move. In otherwards, I bitched out right then. Running away from Evilene's, I realized at that very moment that it wasn't that easy for a twelve-year-old than if I was in my prime. I was still a kid in a grown woman's body; let Chester-The-Child-Molester tell it. It wasn't that I didn't have a backbone or the drive that was needed to bolt through that door; I just froze up like a deer in headlights. I ain't gon' front... my aunt had me in a choke

hold during that time. She even made me nervous to ask to piss when I really had to go! This was like a scene from the movie *Misery*, minus my feet being broken into several pieces.

As I played these different scenarios repeatedly in my head, I thought about why my nerves was so bad all the time. I felt that could have been one of the many reasons why I pee'd in the bed most of the time. She had me shook to a point where I was too afraid to ask the prison guard if I could go to the restroom. So, I just held it until the urge subsided. Well, that's what I thought the piss would do… subside; not end up all around the sides of me soaking up another sheet in exchange for a head-first piss-smothering gesture from the bitch and an ass whooping to top it off! Dayuuuum, I hated that bitch with a muthafuck'n passion, I swear!

Waking up in a chokehold after peeing in the bed from one of those sitting on the toilet dreams never resulted in just a mistake and all forgotten. It would ALWAYS end bad for me. No matter how I tried to give reason to my issue; which was what she called it…. *Reason… Excuses…* At the end of trying to argue my case, I always end up losing. It was useless. *And you know what?* That's what I begin to think about myself all those years… *useless…*

The punishments were always severe to me. There were many options to choose from. An extension cord, backhand across my face, and the list goes on. All of this on this specific day was over my ass forgetting to set the phone back up the way it was. We were forbidden to use her phone for any reason which I eventually had an escape route…my neighbor.

She ended up given me a burner phone, we'll call this device, *"Mufuckas knew some of 'the shit that was going on behind closed doors and felt sorry for auh-bitch."* I had finally had enough and was ready to charge this bitch like a raging bull! I snapped back fast and knew the whole tackle move was just a figment of my imagination, but she had it coming, believe that!

Those were the thoughts that was running through my head as I stared at the front door. It was like the more I pondered on darting through it, never looking back…the bridge I was trying to cross at that moment that would lead me to the other side, *was all in my head.*

In all reality, I had nowhere to fucking go! The more I realized I had nowhere to run too, the further the idea of leaving at that moment got pushed back! And just to think, that was my ticket to freedom.

9
ON LIKE DONKEY KONG

*Now where did I leave off at...*oh shit ok, I remember! Let's rewind a tab bit. I had been sneaking and talking on this burn out phone my neighbor gave me to use when my aunt was gone. My aunt had two phones on a stand in the dining room. The *69 method was Evilene's way of monitoring if the phone had been *messed wit...* LOL (In my *Mista's*, played by *Danny Glover*, voice from one of my favorite films *"The Color Purple")*. Yall know that scene when *Celie*, played by *Whoopi Goldberg*, nervously asked *Mista*, running out to the mailbox with a plate of cookies, to give the postman on the horse after the mail was delivered, she looked up at him and asked, *"Anything for me???"* He gave her this twisted up evil stare and quoted that term above.

Anyhow, the look she had on her face was unforgettable. It had this expression of a pain so deep it cut like a knife. Well, that was the same kind of fear I was experiencing when I heard her making her way to the door! I had no time to put everything back like she had it setup before turning that key to the lock that gained entry to an ass whooping if I didn't get the shit under wraps! I nervously moved so fast that I failed to set everything back up like she had it. The phone cord switch fuck-up..

'Damn, Gina!' (In my *Martin Lawrence voice from the TV show* 'Martin') ... My heart was racing so fast as I darted back to my cell! I just knew and was prepared for the worst that was yet to come...

When she came through the door, my brother Desmond accompanied her into the house. But like the movie, *"Misery,"* she walked in the house looking around for anything to bitch about. She picked up the phone and saw that it was dead, because I plugged in the wrong phone cord rushing. I honestly didn't think the bitch was crazy enough to do anything irrational in front of him. So, I relaxed a little as I sat on the edge of the bed. Desmond walked in my room and said, "Whad'up, sis!" He smiled, preparing to reach out to me. Only a few feet away from me, she flew around and slapped the fuck out of me so hard it knocked the wind out of me! She spat at me maliciously, "You been fuckin with my phones?!"

My bro had to gather his thoughts before asking, "What the fuck just happened, sis?!" As his rotated back and forth between me and my aunt walking away. She did the shit so easily without pause it appeared to be normal to her. I was crying and so angry I was at my wits end!

"FUCK THIS SHIT BRO! I'M GETTING THE FUCK OUT OF HERE! I CAN'T TAKE THIS NO'MOE!" I cried out in anger as I went to throwing my hand-me-downs in this cheap plastic grocery bag that was ripping open from being stretched from my clothing. I was just grabbing shit mainly out of nervousness and confusion at that moment. Even though my brother was there to witness what had just taken place! I couldn't read what he was thinking at the time. I just reacted to whatever happened at that very moment with all the adrenaline I had going on right then!

"Sis, get yo' shit and walk yo' ass out to my car. We out this bitch!"

Though I was anxious, mixed with a little excitement from his reaction, a part of me wasn't secure enough to believe that it was going to be a walk in the park of my departure right at that very moment! I was still scared of the bitch, I ain't gon' lie! So that feeling I was enduring must have been noticeable to him.

"Orlanda… Don't you worry about shit! She ain't gon' touch you! Go'head. Go to the car," he expressed in an urgent tone.

"You ain't said nothin' but a word, bro."

Think about it like this… me, my sister and my baby brother had been held captive up in this bitch for years! Abuse, punishments, and writing thousands of sentences became normal after so long. As a victim of years of abuse, I learned that one grows numb to it, and it becomes a part of where you are and who you are. So that motivation of getting out of there finally after all those years didn't kick in right away. I couldn't taste or touch my freedom right then. I could only see the path to it. And walking that path was like walking the plank which always led to nowhere.

But once my foot hit the porch that led to the sidewalk and into the front seat of his vehicle…oh my God! That feeling of where I was right then in my life I could never forget till this very day! While me and my brother were hopping in the car, my aunt was yelling, "Where you taking her, Desmond?!"

"We just hanging out, auntie. She good wit' me."

He made up some shit while getting the fuck on! I felt loved for the first time in a long time the day I left her home with my bro. Though it took him for fucking ever to check up on me, I was just elated to be up out that bitch! And from that moment moving forward…IT WAS ON LIKE DONKEY KONG!

10
"LIVING IN FEAR"

"YAAAAAAASSSSSSSS!!"

I cried out in joy mixed with a little pain and the feeling of insecurities. I found myself still struggling with a little discomfort after my bro took me to his place of residence. It was a flat off Clairmont, where him and my sister Marlena lived together. As soon as I walked through the door, she greeted me with, "So, I see you ran away, huh?" She looked at me with this look of relief and that happy-to-see-me look on her face waiting on me to respond.

"You already know. I'm never going back," I responded, as I sat my bags of clothes that I snatched up, but should have left. As I placed my raggedy bags that I had stuffed into it on to the floor next to the couch, I was just anxious to catch up and get settled with freedom. My brother and sister instantly went to work on my wardrobe and my hair, and just trying to make me feel at home.

I ain't gon' front like I wasn't afraid of the inevitable. I was still a ward of the State and Evilene did have custody of me. I was not comfortable with that at all. It was like I had escaped prison and was on the run! At any given moment 5.0. could pull up and put me back in harm's way. My little brother was still in foster care so my aunt, aka Evilene, was without me and my siblings to use as a punching bag to let off steam after a day of losing at Bingo!

I really believe to this day her mood was set on the principal of how a day went at Bingo. She had that shit down to a science. When I tell you she could navigate at least 95 plus Bingo boards per drawing; that was her escape from dealing with the evilness of who she was as a human-being. And whenever she was dealing with or had to face the ugliness inside of her, she preyed on me and my siblings by punishing us as a way to feel good about herself. It was like how bullies are; they need to fuck with other mufuckas to take their mind off that monster that exist inside of them. That bitch needed therapy the day she came out of my grandmother's womb. I can't say what her or my mom may have endured under their roof coming up, but whatever was passed on through that generational curse I would always pray it didn't affect me and mine.

Being there with my older siblings after my departure from my aunts, I began to let my guard down a little. It was quiet for a minute until she grew balls and brought her old ass over there to call herself picking me up. Now my sister Marlena said that whenever she found the balls to jump on her broom and fly her ass over there, she was going to beat the shit out of her with it! LOL! I was ready for her ass. She was gon' learn ta-day, in retrospect.

No more Cinderella stories where a prince didn't exist. I was ready for her ass. To think that it would be that easy to throw me in the backseat of her car willingly after getting a taste of freedom was a figment of her imagination. Miss me wit' that shit! That right there wasn't going to get the energy or a response. My life was moving in a different direction from that day forward and balling backwards wasn't an option for me, period!

I knew the legal ramifications that hovered over me and the risk my brother took the day he removed me from her home. He pretty much handled the situation where I was determined to get my life back on track and adjust. I was turning over a new leaf. Though I knew there would be bumps in the road because I didn't really know shit about the streets and being on my own. I spent most of those years where I should have been taught things about the development of transitioning from a girl to a woman with a person that saw the importance of that…but that wasn't the life that was chosen for me obviously.

They say you shouldn't question God for why certain things happen to us out of our control. I guess when I was enduring a lot of this inflicted pain in my life, He wasn't ready to remove me from it. I don't want to believe that a child of innocence like myself was being punished the way I was based on religion. So, I pretty much decided not to challenge that. I'll just let the chips fall where they may.

11
THE UGLY DUCKLING

Finally, my brother had freed me from my abuser. After all the times I felt he had forgotten us, he didn't. He stepped up and moved me into a flat that he had already moved my older sister into, and quickly enrolled me in school after I got settled. Because I was so verbally and physically abused, that shit took a toll on more than just my mental health. My confidence and self-identity were severely distorted. I felt I wasn't the prettiest and it showed. I was a tomboy, so I wore baggy clothes, rarely combed my hair or cared about my physical appearance. The main thing I cared about more than anything at that very moment was getting that muh'fuckin PAPER tho'!

I couldn't just watch my sister Marlena hustling ass making major moves and sit back like a bump on a log, or my brother Desmond doing what he did best while sitting around watching

TV or some shit. I had to pull my weight while still making sure I did my part.

One particular day, my brother broke his triple beam balance scale and couldn't get another one because the place that the "Roc-Boys" got them from was out of stock and didn't expect to have any for about a week. He paced the floor back and forth trying to think of what he was going to do because that scale was an important tool to his business.

He glanced at me with this look on his face, as if he had just discovered electricity. "Orlanda," he said, "don't you have a Science Lab class in school?" "Yeah," I responded, "Good," he proceeded to go into detail about what was on his mind. "When you get to school, I need you to pay close attention when you go to your science class. Peep the scales and plan on going back to class at the end of the day and grabbing one."

"I need you to take your bookbag, stuff a scale in that bitch and bring it home. Make sure you wait until everyone is gone, make sure you get IN AND OUT very quickly, and make sure you zip your bag closed."

I knew I had to do something to help my brother get us by. He broke his triple-beam-balance scale; that was a necessary tool to keeping the money flowing with his street shit. Fuck that, we needed to eat! I went to school, did exactly what he said, and executed the plan to a Tee, I brought the scale home, put that mothafucka' on the table and "BOOM!" I'm officially a street bitch.

Okay so, school wasn't cutting it for me, and I had to make moves and make me some GOTTDAMN MONEY. So, I sold weed for my brother while still not really caring about my appearances at the time. I wasn't the type of bitch that cared about what the next muhfucka thought about me if it didn't yield to some funds. That's real talk!

As far as I was concerned, fuck what another muhfucka thought that wasn't bringing no bread to the table! What I did and how it was done was nobody's business!

As long as we were getting this *money* and making the necessary moves to make shit happen. Everyone else that had an opinion outside of family about my clothes being baggy and my hair wasn't laid, could suck-a-dick! I really didn't care if I was coming or going; it was the bag for me that we were chasing. I hope I made myself clear.

12
"NO NEW FRIENDS" "PUSHED TO A POINT OF NO RETURN"

OMAR
AKA O..

Let me share somethin' with you all... Here I am, forced to grow up, thuggin' it out on my own, finally having my own voice at the tender age of sixteen, I need a fuck'n break, real talk, with this growing up shit! I haven't even experienced being a kid, let alone stepping into womanhood without it being forced on me some kind of way.

Surviving in the streets of Detroit was a hard knock life for us. A lot of the decisions that was made for me being only sixteen was challenging, especially being a ward of the State! I knew my life was gonna be what the fuck it was if I didn't leave this one nigga alone quick! *His name? Omar, a.k.a. "O"* for short, which was what the streets called him. He didn't own no street honors or some shit to be given a nickname. He was just another dumb ass nigga that thought he ran some shit out here in the streets of Detroit with these mediocre muhfucka's that was still living in their mom's basement or sleeping on their homeboy's couch.

Let me move this shit along… Omar and his cousin Rick stayed next door from me, and I had a big ass crush on Rick fine ass first, but because his hating ass cousin Omar was "cock-blocking" and being the jealous, fuck-boy-ass-nigga he was, he pretty much ambushed me into being his girl. Don't ask me how that went over my head at the time, being that I had my eyes on one dick and one dick only and that was Rick wit' the big dick. At least that was the word in the streets from local freaks. Though I realized I had a choice, I went against my first mind and cashed in on this worthless ass nigga instead. I thought after making that mistake, I would never gamble again. Foolish thinking… Anyhow, I ignored that little green man on my shoulder that forbid me against making a decision that could have cost me my life. So, like a pogo-stick, I jumped on tha' dick, LOL! *Laugh now, cry later…*

All jokes aside, I had to laugh to keep from crying at times while with that nigga. That's how sad my situation was. It was the only way I could cope under the circumstances. It took too much of my personal energy to try and like him, yet alone love him, which with all the abuse he inflicted on me, was short-lived.

Just to elaborate on this subject a little more, I can't honestly say I ever really loved him. I would be cheating myself if I said I shared an inch of love for this dummy. I take that love shit serious being that it only comes around once or twice in a lifetime. Unfortunately, I didn't experience those emotions with him. But, just to add humor to a traumatic situation, he did get the opportunity to take my breath away a couple times throughout that relationship. Sad to say, but those times were when he wrapped his deadly paws with claws around my neck with the intent to kill my ass! At least that's how I felt. Like death awaited.

I hated that nigga with a passion. The bullshit I went through with him was unforgivable and unforgettable. Though I knew it had to be a God watching over me each time I made it to see another day. I was favored and put through many tests throughout the many phases in my life. Though some may feel I should have been used to being abused, it took that experience with O to witness the different phases of it.

Ultimately, I wanted my freedom from this evil being. I spent seconds to minutes, and minutes to hours, contemplating on the opportunity to escape death that stood in the shadows of evilness. Just to share some of the selfishness of a person who didn't give a fuck about my dreams, my needs or what I desired in life, I'll never forget this time he made me come over his house to cook him some breakfast before going to school. This arrogant mufucka had to have his drawls on backwards to think I was that bitch. Like his shit was all the way together to have any woman that had goals and a desire to graduate, that would have rather been at school than standing over a stove for his hoe ass! That shit rubbed me the wrong way! Fuck-nigga! He was out for self.

Dude forced me into a few situations I wish I never had to do like having sex with him when I didn't want to for the most part. On some real shit legally, that was considered rape! I was only in the beginning stages of high school when we connected. On some high-risk, not giving-a-fuck shit because the nigga had me so heated this day… I grew some balls and was fed up with all the abuse and disrespect to a point of no return. So, because I was on some not-giving-a-fuck-shit my crazy ass went and spoke to another dude that got my attention in front of this nigga. I knew it was a suicide move but fuck that nigga! And sho'nuff, "O" bitch ass smacked the shit out of me with a 2-liter pop bottle in front of everybody. I was so embarrassed. I hated that nigga!

Shit like that happened between us on a regular basis. I remember I had had enough of his abuse, so I broke up with him over the phone. His response was him letting me know he was going to fuck me up when he saw me. Later that day I ended up going down the street to my homegirl house. She stayed on the corner by the alley. As I was standing there talking to her, this crazy mf comes out of the alley on my ass like the Black Ops!

He hit me with so much force, it knocked me over the side of her porch into some sticker bushes that pierced through my flesh like pins! I was in so much pain, I swear. It was excruciating! He fucked me up bad. My homegirl instantly jumped to my defense, "Stop hitting that girl like that!" She couldn't do shit! I wanted out, but it was dangerous levels to that shit, bro. It seemed like the more I tried, I died inside. There were so many incidents.

The final straw was the time he knocked my ass down these flight of steps at this two-family flat we were at! Just to give you a visual on how it was set up, think about a two-family flat home where the stairs go straight up to the top and there was a door that stood between you and those steps that when you turn around, it's like one of those Demon-Drop ride feelings you see at an amusement park from the depths of it.

I wasn't expecting to get my wig split this day. Especially a nigga crazy enough to knock me down a flight of steps that high up! That was an understatement, and down I went over some bullshit he was on! I never touched a step as my body flew through the air like Wonder-Woman without a cape! Now yall know she need the muhfuckn' cape to fly right?! When he heard how hard I hit the ground, he ran down after me. He saw the damage he had done and proceeded to react by punching out the glass window on the screen door. The glass ended up splitting his arm completely open to the white meat! Blood was pouring out of his arm like a faucet. His people must've heard all the commotion, because shortly after his cousin ran to his aid, wrapped his arm in a towel, then they rushed him to the hospital.

That was the straw that broke the camel's back! I was on a mission to get ghost on his ass before he buried me. His arm was damaged way more than I expected. He ended up losing all use of it. It was shriveled and basically a dead limb. I was able to get my shit and slide out while he was still in the hospital. We're talking about an asshole-nutcase ass nigga who didn't give a fuck about what the police and anyone else who had an opinion had to say! He was a ready-to-die nigga! So, tell me how the fuck was I going to survive from that shit?

It was hard being with a jealous hearted nigga who had no real desire to live. Women were pawns… a piece of shit to him. It was obvious the nigga had mommy issues which I can almost guarantee he was beating her ass too! The abuse wasn't going to stop. I didn't have my brother or no male figures around at the time to defend me. This was during the time my brother, Desmond, was locked up. So, I was pretty much on my own. It was me against the world. And after I finally found my way of out that maze it was game over. I was granted parole from that nigga… he was a figment of my imagination!

Eventually, O got caught up on some dumb shit that ultimately broke that chain, and I was out…never looking back! I remember having conversations with a few seasoned older men and women I came across whom I respected their opinions. They opened my eyes to how people, situations, and circumstances from your past can come back to haunt you if you are in your weakest vulnerable moment in life. It's like a gateway to re-enter if you're not aware of your surroundings. You could easily leave that back door open to your future subjecting you to lose sight of what once existed that held you mentally and physically incapacitated. If you're not mindful and aware of some of the things and beings that were considered a test you went through, they will be able to revisit, *causing you more damage than good.*

Years later this dude reached out to me about a blast from my past that I never wanted to relive... You guessed it... *O!* He sent a message of an apology wanting to somehow jumpstart this relationship of what I can describe as a locked-up engine on an old truck I threw away years ago. The first thing came to mind was, "hell naw! I didn't need no apology, no gifts and no messenger to approach me with it! I just needed that nigga to crawl back up in his hole and pull the dirt back over it. That part of my life is dead, and I meant that shit. No new friends!

13
"VICTIMS OF THE SYSTEM"

Let's talk about my parents, and how we even ended up at Aunt Evilene's house in the first place. It's like a broken record when you go into the back stories of many Black African Americans. Drug addicted parents, poverty and neglect was like a broken record. The story of my siblings and I was no different. All in the same fucked up category, different black family, same story.

Both of my parents were on drugs. Because of their neglect, we were taken from the home. I don't know if it was divine intervention, or a cruel joke, but we ended up being placed in a foster home three blocks away from my Aunt Evilene's house. We thought, "hey, she's family; she'll protect us until our parents come back for us." We ran away from the foster home and knocked on her door. The rest was a horrific history. The only interest she had in me and my baby brother, James Jr., II was a check. So, whenever she was having a bad day, that was an asswhooping moment. Losing to Bingo…beat down! We were her human-punching bags, objects not worth the love and affection warranted to us. There was no love lost…

Why did she take away our innocence? I cried many times in silence.

I found myself talking to myself more than often. Sounds like a bitch was losing her mind at times…not at all; I was very sane. This was a coping mechanism I found myself utilizing often to keep my head right. Though I was the second from the youngest sibling, I thought outside the box. That was my way in looking forward to another day. Survival to its fullest under that fuck'n roof. It was like being on death row with no date to die. You just waking up into another day, wondering what was standing behind Door Number FUCK-THIS-SHIT.

I realized at that point that if Desmond hadn't rescued me when he did, I would've been on an episode of that TV Series *Killer Kids*, from the ID Channel. Evilene would have definitely caught a knife to the chest in her sleep; and that's FACTS!

Just when I became comfortable after being rescued from that torture chamber, my aunt felt invincible by popping up where I was residing with my siblings, Marlena and Desmond, all uninvited trying to plead her case! That shit she was spittin fell on death ears! She had absolutely no idea she was 2-seconds away from an ass-whoopin' that I honestly was looking forward too! I had VIP seats on that shit. Where I stood when that confrontation went down was priceless! My sister, Marlena wasn't for no games. That was baby Ali! Marlena was about that life!

Little did our aunt know, my sister was ready to cash in on dat' ass, on site! *What people do for money*; I swear! Her goal was to bully her way into getting those checks back rolling with the threats and the screaming and yelling! Bye FELICIA! It was blatantly obvious my aunt didn't give a fuck about us! I just stood off to the side listening to the back-and-forth thinking, *"hell naw, you evil bitch! I was all the way good being away from that jail cell you had us locked up in all those years! Beat it!"*

My mind was spinning the whole time they stood there yelling. I felt secure that my sister was not going to lose that argument and give in! There was NO going back!

Miss me wit' that shit, BLACK PATTY!

All I could think about was how good I had it living with my older siblings. That taste of genuine love and freedom since I moved in with them and being in the company of their friends made me feel for once like I was a part of a family. Not to mention, I was making a few dollars on the side with my hustles. There's NO FUCKIN' WAY I'd be going back to the Amityville House to continue to be fucked by my abusers.

So, when Evilene refused to leave one other time she popped up having the audacity to try to put up a fight. Her ass got turned right the fuck around again. Every attempt she got straight ignored. She even tried to petition to get my little brother back after she brutalized him! She was trying every possible way she could to secure another check since she had lost custody of us. But her time was DONE. No more checks, no more punching bags! Custody was turned over to Marlena following the payments which were reversed and transferred shortly after.

My sister and I ended up moving to Highland Park. Not too long after that my little brother, James, ended up popping up at our door shortly after running away from the home he was placed in. We, of course welcomed him with open arms and thugged that shit out together. That's when the next phase of our lives continued…

14

"LOVE DON T PAY THE BILLS"

Once I turned 17, I was already pregnant with my son. I was pretty much an adult in my eyes. I was taking care of myself and making my own money. I was still staying with my sister when I met my son's father. He was staying with his mother, who just so happened to be a crazy ass Jehovah's Witness. You know, those believers who knock on your door early as hell on the weekends asking if you had a friend in Jesus. Listen, I'm not religious at all, so any religion that consists of not celebrating any holidays, never caught my attention.

Due to their religious beliefs, my boyfriend and I weren't allowed to sleep together. As in the same bed. We were clearly way past that given the fact I was already well into my pregnancy. So, we were definitely "sleeping together," and then some. We found other ways around her rules of course. We'd spend the night together at this animal food store that my uncle ran. My baby daddy would help him out around the store for a couple dollars here and there. We'd sleep there in the back on top of some big ass bags of hay, dog food or whatever we could find to cushion our asses. On the nights that we couldn't stay there, we'd stay at my sister's house.

Since I got out in the streets, I experienced a different way of living. Some consisting of the way I would cushion my own bag. So, after so long, I just couldn't get with the broke shit. All this nigga wanted to do was play basketball while I stayed at home playing broke. Fuck that shit. I eventually had to get it how I lived. He would be out all fucking day doing his recreational shit that never yield to no funds! Nigga, where they do that at? I was fucking irritated after so long. Falling out of love with his ass eventually became easy. That was just some shit I couldn't get with. I had to get the fuck on ASAP (in my Black Chyna mama Tokyo Toni voice).

One day when I was at home, my "spidey" senses started tingling. Something in my mind told me this nigga had me fucked up and couldn't be trusted. I ended up pressing redial on the house phone to see who this nigga had been talking to or calling. Of course, some bitch picked up the phone spilling the beans about fucking my broke ass baby father. I was so fuckin pissed, I blacked out! I can't remember what I said to the hoe. I just remember packing up all me and my son's shit. Without his knowledge, I took everything. Furniture and all. His ass ain't pay for shit fah'real anyway. I was done with the bum.

Of course, when a real bitch leaves a nigga, they wanna turn crazy. Just become reckless and out of control. When I left him, I moved back with my sister and what this nigga do??? This fool continuously pursued and harassed me whenever he saw me over there. I wasn't going for that shit at all, you feel me? He was a complete turn off to me. Once you show me you're not capable of leading, I'm no longer interested. Just like that, I shut down. What's that saying? "I can do bad all by myself." Which left that nigga no room for fucking up.

Now I'm not a petty bitch. I allowed him to see his son whenever he attempted to get him, but that was it. Of course things got worse with him after that. It's like the farther down he fell, the crazier he got. Which I couldn't understand the shit. I had already moved on and had started dating this nice guy when my son was about 6/7 months old. We had just started kick'n it and was about to head out on a date. He picked me and my baby up and we headed over to my BD mother's house to drop my son off for the evening. *Why did I do that?!?*

I walked up to the porch and brought my son and his overnight bag and put them both in the house. My BD didn't notice I pulled up with a guy until I left out the house and got back in the car. When he peeped dude, he fucking lost it! Do yall know this hoe ass nigga put my son and all his clothes and belongings in the middle of the sidewalk. I just picked my baby up and bussed up on his ass. There were years between us before I had ever asked that bitter bitch for anything. We good over here homie! Believe that!

15
"MAKE THAT MONEY... DON T LET THE MONEY MAKE U..."

Fantasia, my dance alter ego was born when I was about 18/19 years old. with my older sister. Of course, I didn't like it. I mean come on... That's not like going to a job interview at Mc Donald's and stripping down to a G-String to flip burgers. On top of dealing with my trauma with physical and sexual abuse, it just wasn't me. But, as I made a few attempts and let my guard down, little- by-little it started helping me with my confidence, no lie.

    I found myself tapping into my sex appeal. You know that alter ego inner bad bitch side. It was on and pop'n then! The money was falling in my lap and from that point on, it was giving me this motivation I never knew I had. I was different from the more seasoned bitches. I was unique, which should have been my dance name. But, Fantasia fit the profile because that bitch was a monster on the fucking stage. Hell, I could slide up and down on that pole like I owned it. I had my own swag that set me apart from the others. I didn't fraternize or socialize too much. I made my money, stacked my chips and bounced.

Now my sister ended up dancing at a spot called "The Wood 6" where you could walk in there on damn near any day of the week and make a killing! Now, the place was nasty as fuck, and it disgusted me as soon as I stepped in that bitch like clockwork. One thing fasho was I couldn't front tho', the bread was falling in my lap every time I stepped in the building. The money was too good and coming too fast. A muh'fuckn 9 to 5 couldn't pay me nothing compared to what the strip club was paying! It didn't take long at all to rope me in. They say money is the root of all evil, and that's when my confidence shot through the roof. Dancing at the strip club in the city was a stepping-stone for me especially in the white strip clubs.

As the music roared through the bar…

"Gone shake dat ass… Imma get this money… Gon' shake dat ass, Imma get this money!" I crooned the words to this song as I stepped up in the club. Though the music and atmosphere were a bit different, none of that shit mattered when it came to *Benny's* old wrinkled up face on hunned's falling in my lap. Just rain on a bitch, why don't-cha!

My off days people didn't know what I did to get money besides sell weed or they assumed I had a rich nigga breaking me off. Nah, this wasn't that at-tall…. I was on a need-to-know basis wit Mufuka's. They didn't know I was a dancer because I didn't carry myself as such. So, I continued to allow those who had their nose up in my ass trying to figure me out, continue to make their assumptions and have their opinions. Before they could figure shit out, my life was on a role to making more money than a Big-3 check. I learned the game and mastered it. There was no turning back. The Ugly Duckling was on the road to becoming an official Bad Bitch, First Class!

Before I jumped into the field headfirst, Marlena used to throw parties for a whole bunch of paid people from all around the city. I was able to dance because it was a private setting and mostly only the people she knew. The parties would get wild sometimes. There weren't many rules put in place, so people just did whatever they wanted. It wasn't long before I was introduced to the Titty Bar. It was my homegirl, Berry, who showed me the ins and outs of that world.

The first bar I ever worked at was on Plymouth and Southfield, smack dab in the middle of the hood. You can only imagine the atmosphere. I was there for only about a year. I didn't really like working at black bars. I was a slim girl number one. Not the "Big Booty Judy" type bitch at all. It wasn't long until I found my place among the "non-melanated" bar scene. Better security and environment, way more money, less effort. What else could a natural born hustler ask for? Let's not forget, no shoot-outs, unnecessary cat fights or bitches stealing everything but the bloody tampon you just pulled out your pussy! A breath of fresh air.

I took my hustle nationwide. I loved to travel, so doing so to make my coins was always a plus. Being surrounded by middle-aged and older foreign and white men gave me nothing but space and opportunity. I wasn't a dance all day, working fulltime type of broad. I like to bag 'em and tag 'em. In and out. Get up on about $1000-$1500 and I'm out until the next time I need to rake up some bread. Run Me My MONEY!

I saw a lot of shit in the business. From girls getting strung out on drugs, to girls getting pimped out and even worse…girls coming up missing or found dead. That type of unfortunate circumstance made me uncomfortable. The shit was crazy! Which forced me to have second thoughts about what I was doing. I really believed after so long I grew tough skin. Shit around me bounced off me as you get used to what eventually became normal.

One thing fa'sho' was I loved being my own boss, working for myself. Which meant making my own money. Only the strong survived in the stripper game. I remember raking in 15K at one of my B-Day parties which was the most I made in one night. I was on top of the world this particular time! Only the strong survive in the stripper game. One thing for sure was I loved dancing at the white bars mainly because they wasn't as boujie. The people that stopped in these kinds of bars wasn't too picky. They didn't really make you feel uncomfortable as I'd seen at other bars in the inner city. They were laid back and I hardly ever ran into people I knew personally. What was crazy was many people I bumped into never knew what I did for a living. In my circle people thought I sold drugs or had a stable filled with suga-daddies. I think people had their own perception of me because of how I carried myself. I didn't come off like I stripped! This may be one of the many reasons why I am so happy those days are behind me.

16

"I AIN'T NO KILLA, BUT DON'T PUSH ME"

Coming from where I'm from, carrying a gun is like carrying a purse. It's an accessory. Shit, better yet, a necessity. I carried a gun with me everywhere I'd go. I had to! I was doing a lot better for myself. I'm in my early twenties now, slightly more established, more mature, I just felt like THAT BITCH. I dealt with this dude that worked at this rental car place, so he kept me plugged in with whatever whips I wanted. He kept me in The New Cadillac DTS and Deville for two years straight. I switched the colors like I switched my panties. It was like that! These hoes couldn't stand me! I stayed with my foot on their neck. I had condos in these bitches' heads as much as I stayed on these bitches minds! HA! Me and my home girl. She had the Cadi Truck as well, so the flex was real ok.

Me and my home girl decided to switch trucks one day and hang out downtown. I was looking good as fuck in her Caddy truck. Obviously too good because this guy I met down there was all over me. Crushing real hard, selling dreams that a bitch like me could more than afford to get for myself. But he was cute though, so I played the game with him. I ended up meeting him at his house the following day for a little sip and smoke session. He stayed over there off Fenkell and Hubbell. You know, by Cooley High School on the westside of Detroit.

So anyway, I make it to his house. We chilling; he pours me a drink and we vibing. The entire time we are talking, his phone is ringing off the chain. I was thinking to myself, either this nigga a drug dealer, or he got a bitch. After the phone rings for the 15th time, I ask him if he would like to be excused to answer his phone, no pressure. That must've made him feel a little too comfortable because this nigga says it's his whole girlfriend blowing up his phone right now. Niggas ain't shit, I tell you.

But here's the punchline. While this muhfucka got me here at his house and his girlfriend blowing up his phone. This muhfucka got TWO MORE women outside circling the block trying to catch him up, all at the same damn time. This type of drama ain't for me baby so I had to Cha Cha Slide my ass right on out of there! Plus, I'm from the 'I wish a bitch would,' *you feel me*?

After I finished my drink, I politely put out my cigarette and told ol' boy it was time for me to skate. As he's walking me to the door, I peep the two girls who were stalking his house had decided to block my truck in with their cars in front of the driveway. This particular day, like every day, I had that NINA on me. I'm not about to play with no niggas OR bitches today! As I'm coming down the driveway I calmy drew my gun and them bitches scattered like roaches in the kitchen when the light comes on. I jumped in my truck and got the hell on. I never saw that nigga again. Rock-a-bye baby.

17
DON'T TEST MY GANGSTA

I had finally been living in my own shit for a while now. It was a Family Flat on Clairmont and Dexter. It wasn't in the best neighborhood, but it was mine. All mines. It would've been a perfect experience if I didn't have to deal with my ghetto ass hating ass neighbors. They reminded me of this show I be watching now called Neighbors from hell, except they tried the wrong muhfucka. See I don't play that disrespect shit. What made it even worse is that they didn't like me for a nonexistent reason. Just hating and jealous clearly. It's hard to tell a mf not to poke the bear, when they don't know it's a bear they're poking.

My neighbors stayed downstairs while I had the upstairs flat. They would do little petty shit all the time to try to irritate me with loud ass noises and music while my son and I are trying to sleep, slick remarks and comments under their breath while I'm passing. Just ugly bitch shit. Hater shit. But I chose to ignore it because queens don't stoop to the level of peasants, but after this particular day, oh shit was about to hit the fan.

One day in particular I came home, and them hoes mf big ass pit bull was in my house! Ask me how that muhfucka got in there, the jury is still out on that. Strike one!

Next scenario. A few months later, I was invited to a party by a good friend of mine. Of course, I had to look fly, so I went and bought me some crispy ass K Swiss to wear. I left them upstairs in MY HOUSE, then left back out to find an outfit and some accessories. When I came home, not only were my fuckin K Swiss gone, BUT my damn TV was ALSO gone as well! That was strike two, FUCK a strike three! I was on their ass! They had me all the way bent and clearly thought I was a weak bitch and could and would not stand with me! Ima Muhfuckin' Shaw, bitch!

I called all my niggas from the hood! They ride for me and was ready to mangle everybody in that mf house. It was about fifteen of my niggas on the porch ready for war. The only reason I canceled that royal ass beat down that was about to commence, was because there was a child in the house. A little boy. That's against my code. I don't fuck with kids. I called off the dogs that time, but them bitches got the point and was church mouse quiet from then on.

I ended up seeing him again at the **IHOP** off Dequindre and 696. There was a strip of hotels over there and I just so happened to be at the one directly across the street from his. I was alone, but I was strapped. This one was a different piece though, with a silencer. He didn't recognize me, but I peeped his ass.

I sat in the car and watched him and the young lady he was with walk over to the hotel he was at. This nigga was slipping. I could've bodied his ass without a second thought. Poof, gone! God was on his side though because I just went on about my day. I had something for his ass later though.

I killed time until darkness fell. When I was sure I could be "incognegro", I made my way over to his hotel. I found the car I saw him driving and proceeded to shoot that mf up. Straight Swiss cheesed it. Thanks to the silencer on my gun, I was able to take out all four tires and windows without someone noticing. I hopped back in my car and hit the freeway. I found pleasure in thinking about the look on his face when he saw his whip. That's what you get for stealing from me, bitch! LOL.

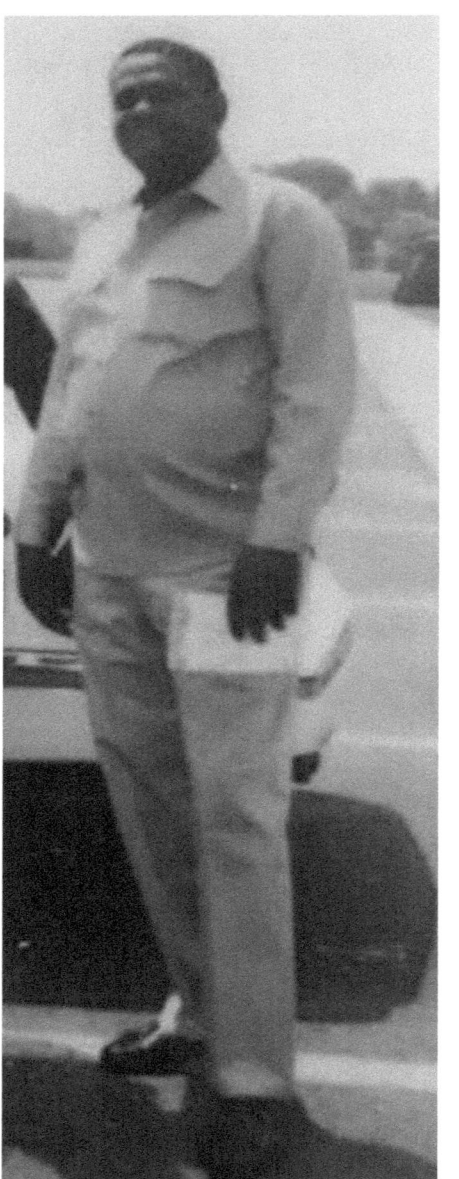

18
"POPPA WAS A PLAYA"

My father, or "Pops" as we called him was a pretty humble man. He was from a pretty large family, the baby boy of his siblings but he was by far, the toughest. In that regard, I guess you could say, he was the "BIG" little brother. Jr. as he was affectionately known (named after his father) was a WILD BOY growing up and as life would have it, he became a WILD MAN. Not formally educated, my father was a "Hustler." He could play the game with them best of them, and as life would have it, as with most "hustlers" of his era, Drugs became the "go to" when things got rough and they needed to cope.

Both of my parents were indeed on drugs, but my father came out of that shit. Our relationship was nonexistent until after my son was born. It seemed like that opened a door to form some sort of bond between us. Not to mention, I was dropping big bucks off to my dad when I started doing well for myself. So, I'm almost sure that had a lot to do with it.

Anyway, I adore my father. All of us do. We looked up to him. He was THAT NIGGA back in the day. Not only was he that nigga, but he was also a real ass PIMP. I'm talking about an official, bitches on the payroll ass pimp. He stayed throwing live ass gambling parties for the paid niggas around the way. They'd come party, chill, and fuck on their dimes; not his of course.

I still see some of his hoes till this day around the way. Stayed speaking to them, showing them mad respect, and looking out for them when I can. My father wasn't the best dad, but he taught me a lot and I appreciate him for that. My dad always dropped gems on us growing up. Kept us street smart; gave us the real, raw, and uncut. He was always very serious, but a gentle giant at the same time.

It killed me when he died. Only a few months after I moved to Florida. In the back of my mind, I always thought that if only I hadn't moved, he would still be here. That was one of the saddest and depressing times for me. I took the loss of my father very hard. I can still hear him talking to me sometimes. I hear his voice clear as day.

One thing about my father's passing that changed me is the fact that he left us nothing. I have a son, and I would never want that for him. I already have a life insurance policy on myself set in place for my son. Not only that though, I wanted more for him. More generational wealth set in place. I wanted to make sure my son was GOOD if anything had ever happened to me. That's when I knocked over the first domino to the Shaw legacy. I will always love my father and am eternally grateful for him raising my son to be the man he is today.

19
"FLESH OF MY FLESH, BONE OF MY BONE"

I know that being a mother isn't everybody's forte. Some people can adapt and master the responsibility. Some can't. A mother's love is one of the most influential and wholesome feelings in a child's life. It's a necessity above all other things. It's the mother's heart beat a baby hears for the first nine months while growing inside the stomach. Her voice is the first voice the baby hears. Her face, the first face a baby's lays its eyes on. That is spiritual on top of genetics. A mother's love is the closest thing to feeling God's love.

Now MY mama was a muhfucka! Strung out on drugs, tricking, disappearing for long periods of time. This has been my mother for my whole life. I don't remember her ever being any other way. I thought this shit was normal until I saw how other kid's moms loved and cared for them. No mommy and me days, no quality time. Shit, she didn't even teach me anything about being a girl, periods, hygiene, NOTHING. She didn't cook for us, hug us, I don't even remember her telling me she love me! How fucked up is that?

No matter how my mother abused me mentally, emotionally, and verbally, I refused to disrespect her though. I loved my mother with all of me and always made excuses for her. Maybe she was abused too. Maybe the demon she was battling was too powerful. I know my mom loved me. She had to. I was her daughter. Flesh of her flesh, bone of her bone. I just told myself mentally she couldn't love me right, she didn't even love herself. I forced myself to believe that.

The older I got our relationship stayed stagnant. All the things she needed my brother provided. Her personals, toiletries, and money for her pockets. Shit, even her cigarettes and liquor, so luckily that pressure wasn't always on me. There would be times I'd be riding through the neighborhood and I'd run into my mom tricking. I'd just roll down the window and yell out, "Ma! Get your butt in this car girl!" Unfortunately, our dialogue between each other wasn't that of a mother and daughter. More of a homegirl type of feel. Like a "Hey Bitch" "was sup hoe" thing. Crazy right? Shit, not to me, normal asf, you feel me??

I had become uncomfortable with enabling her addiction as well. I don't know why but this one specific time I decided to hold out when she asked me for some money for the millionth time. She came over to my place asking for $20 for whatever reason she made up. I told her "I'm sorry, ma, I don't have it today." Girl, why did I do that shit? She went Donkey Kong on my ass. Obviously, she was tryna get her a fix because I became all type of dirty whores, stripper bitch and trick hoes, lol. It's not funny, but going through the shit I've been through, you learn to develop tough skin. By now, shit my skin made of diamond. Can't no words penetrate this armor.

Having said all of that, I now understand how the combination of both drugs and mental health can devastate a family and cause long term trauma on the children, I am a true product of that deadly combination. While I don't place blame on anyone, I feel that life can be taken for granted by those who lack the understanding.

My mother was the baby girl in her family, and her family was large. My aunts and uncles have never been close and so my picture of family is a little distorted. I didn't have the traditional family values growing up, I didn't know what that even was. Shit, I didn't know what a traditional family looked or felt like. All I've ever known was how to survive. Momma didn't teach me that, she forced me to learn it.

20
"GHETTO LOVE STORY"

Quick backstory on where it all started. My parents met in the 1960's in what they called the Black Bottom area. It wasn't long before my dad, who was a hood entrepreneur, swept my mom off her feet and upgraded her. Not only was he throwing some of the best game and card parties in the neighborhood, he also was a certified PIMP. That didn't get in the way of my mother and him falling in love.

Now that I think of it, my father couldn't stand Auntie Evilene. He even had a nick name for her: Karen Joe The Neighborhood Hoe, LOL. Maybe that's why my auntie abused us. Her hate and jealousy towards my mom and dad were obvious. The fact that my mom had someone to financially support her and her kids while my auntie had to struggle and play bingo to feed her and hers. Makes sense to me.

Back to my parents. Now when the drugs kicked in, shit went left quick. They started being home less and less. The responsibility of taking care of us kids and the household started to fall onto my older sister Marlena. It got to the point where we barely saw them, and we were always hungry and just straight abandoned. CPS was called and we were taken out of the home. The rest is history.

Although my father eventually had gotten clean, my mother stayed on the path of destruction. She succumbed to years of addiction and not taking care of herself. She didn't overdose, but the damage done to her body from her avid drug use was the cause of her death. I still loved my mother with all of me. I still do. I just really wished she could've made a change before God called her home in 2005. I wish she could've known my son and been a part of his life like my father was. I always wondered how life would've been if my mom wasn't on drugs. Would we have had those moments I dreamed of as a child? How would life had turned out for me? Let me stop before I drive myself insane.

My father passed years after my mom in 2019. I thank God that we were able to find common ground before his passing. He really stepped up as a grandfather to my son and for that I thank him. My son has grown to be an amazing man. Generous, educated, humble and respectful; all thanks to having real love and support surrounding him. My parents may have fell short in raising us, but their contributions to my life still had value to me. I pray that they have finally found peace. I love you mom and dad. Rest peacefully and continue to watch over us.

21
"I HAD A DREAM"

You know, I'm sure every human being has experienced having a dream. A dream of becoming a movie star! A Dream of becoming the next Cardi B. HELL!.... Maybe even a dream of living to see the next 200 years!

Ok, now let's focus on the reality of it all, the difference between a dream and a dreamer... A dream is a series of thoughts, images, and sensations occurring in a person's mind during sleep. A dreamer is a person who dreams or is dreaming. Now let me share with you how all of this played a major role in the woman I am today and how it *personally* affected and impacted my life.

Me and seventy-seven other students were chosen to be a part of this phenomenal program back in my 5th grade year while attending Roosevelt Elementary School in Detroit. I can attest to the fact that this was a lifetime opportunity being introduced by this married couple that I'll call *"The Corvilles"*. It was right before we graduated, they thugged it out with all of us. Being that many of us came from all kinds of walks of life, I can assure you this was a challenge for this little Caucasian couple that fit right in with us degenerates. At least that's how many outside our race viewed inner city kids like us. *Fucked up right?*

Well, that's how shit was where I was from; judgement is made before acknowledgement. Let me stay on track… Fucking weed starting to mess with my brain cells. LOL!

They called us dreamers, which was a nickname for the program that follows us to this very day. This was a foundation they set up called, the *"I Have A Dream"* Foundation. This was an opportunity of a lifetime that impacted my life personally for which I can attest too. Mr. Corville was very disciplined and educated in his background of this field, which one would have to have years of experience with children. I can honestly say that our lives throughout this process was changed drastically. Though there were major personal challenges that affected many of us differently, some of us, including myself, was broken and came from harsh and traumatic environments. That alone set us up on a path to confront those demons that had us in a choke hold for the most part.

It honestly felt good to be around others like me, we were like a family, though I didn't get a chance to complete this program, I was armed with many tools that I could incorporate at any time when my life would break down on the side of the road like a burnt-out engine with miles ran over. This was a total package program that gave us stability, hope, and an opportunity to pave a different path than the one we were on. I met some really good people that are still present in my life today. I incorporated so many of the things I've learned.

So many years have flown by, but many of us stayed in touch by throwing picnics and more after. It was always breathtaking to see them after so many years. Though I had some regrets of not following through, I always felt this level of completing something in my life every time I was in the company of those who did. That said a lot about the kind of person I am. I was secure enough within myself to be happy for others that followed through on their endeavors. I was never a hater; I was a motivator entangled with being a congratulator.

This was one of the reasons why I considered myself a humanitarian, by giving back and helping others. This program was nurturing and that came naturally for me. I commend other's success because I was confident with my own, whether it was progressing in the many ventures I had my hands in, or going out and speaking to the youth or young women in several programs all over Detroit and the surrounding areas to share my own personal experiences with the hopes that it would impact their lives the way it did mine.

It was not only important, and a given to know that there were people out there that gave a fuck about a bunch of kids that came from broken homes, abuse, born addicts… the list goes on. Though many in the world I came from looked down on us, labeling us; which was humiliating. I never accepted anything that belittled my character. I matured past that. At a young age I breathed in knowledge and strategically figured out ways to stay one step ahead of the game, whichever way it was played.

This was one of the many tools I stored in my mental rolodex from this program that I was able to implement into writing my life story. I don't think I could have done this without the advantage of Becoming a "Dreamer". The program gave me hope and ways to cope, keeping me grounded and focused long enough when everything around me was falling apart. It was the glue that gave me the understanding and skillset needed of how to put the pieces of my life back together throughout this writing process, which would in essence keep each one of the chapters of my life locked in solid.

There was, and still is a calculated move behind every step I make in my life 'till this very day. I stay mentally and emotionally prepared for whatever move my opponent is strategically planning or sizing me up on. They call this "One Step Ahead of the Game." Like a baby born with an extra finger and six toes, I was unique…gifted to subconsciously have eyes in the back of my head. I could see shit full circle.

Like that boss bitch *Raquel "Raq" Thomas* in *50 Cent's* TV series *Kanan* . I had street/hood smarts, and I didn't play no fucking childish as games. Now I was not as brutal and reckless as she was with that TV animated Gangsta shit she was on, knocking niggas off and shit… not that I would admit to it if I was. This is what I meant by having eyes in the back of my head. The public school system and the way it was set up couldn't keep a boss bitch like myself attention too long before I had to cut ties by not going all the way with it.

I learned more in my 5th grade year with the Dreamer's than I did in those eight hours a day boring ass classes they bounced us around in. What sense did it make to feed my mind with the idea of wanting to graduate to work for a mufucka when it made more sense to take the entrepreneur role and work for myself? Answer that shit, why don't cha'! Fucking mental slavery and I wasn't built for that. I always had to get it how I lived. That was my motivation, and I carried no regrets with the fact that I didn't invest a full 12 years of my life allowing the school system to teach me different. I graduated with "Street Smarts". I wasn't playing any games with those who wasn't on my level. I had real goals and strong missions in life that I was destined to complete.

So, this is not the end of this story by far. I got plenty more shit to say which a college couldn't have paved that road for me. So, while religious people were toting Bibles as their protection and the Muslims embraced the Holy Quran to stimulate their minds…me? I was pack'n 9's.

It's a dirty game out here when you come from the life I'm from. The sad thing was the fact that the same mufuckas you been around all your life would cross you faster than a stranger you've only known for a short period of time! Don't get me wrong, I will always show love and have love for those I'm close to whether its blood or water. To keep it 100, this phase of my life I gave you a taste of is far from the end and where I am from and what I've been through right here, right now.

It's dramatic to its fullest. But I'm not sure I'm ready to release that best right now so I'm going to fizzle this out right here… got a lot more shit to share and say! I'll add that I am still a work in progress and at this phase in my life I know this may seem like I didn't learn shit about what I was taught in this program, but I assure you, my mind, body and soul are fed heavily with enough of my life experiences that would carry me another 40-plus years.

I'm like a sponge. I absorb and wring out all the excessive content, that in essence, is taking up mental space. I'm constantly tying myself into uplifting projects and surrounding myself with those who share similar visions that I do. I don't just sit at the table with you to feed my spirit, while you're transferring dialogue that could be useful, I'm playing in my phone. Naw… I am a realist… And everything you read thus far was real-life-shit.

So, you decide what you want to do with the information and profound dialogue I shared with you throughout my life's journey. If what you read didn't reach or teach you from my experience… then you are an entirely different kind of being that I honestly haven't crossed paths with. One who lacks empathy, emotions and like me, still have more to learn in life. I assure you that this is not the end. My life's journey is just beginning. Can't say I didn't warn you upfront that ya' girl, *Orlando Shaw* is and will always be a never-ending story…STAY TUNED!!!

Ingram Content Group UK Ltd.
Milton Keynes UK
UKHW051241210623
R3360200001B/R33602PG423486UKX00001B/1